The Country I Remember

The Country I Remember

poems

David Mason

Story Line Press / *1996*

Story Line Press; Three Oaks Farm; Brownsville, OR 97327

This publication was made possible thanks in part to the generous support of the
Nicholas Roerich Museum, the Andrew W. Mellon Foundation, the National
Endowment for the Arts, and our individual contributors.

Book design by Chiquita Babb
Cover and Jacket Photograph: "Scenic Overlook" by James Conaway, © 1988

Library of Congress Cataloging-in-Publication Data
Mason, David, 1954–
    The country I remember : poems / David Mason.
      p.   cm.
    ISBN 1-885266-20-0. — ISBN 1-885266-23-5 (pbk.)
    1. United States—History—Civil War, 1861–1865—Poetry.
  2. Soldiers—United States—Poetry. I. Title.
  PS3563.A7879C68 1996
  811.54—dc20   95-52442
                                      CIP

Acknowledgments

Some of these poems first appeared in the following periodicals: *The American Scholar*, "A
Motion We Cannot See"; *The Dark Horse*, "Land Without Grief" and "The Pond"; *The
Hudson Review*, "The Country I Remember" (all), "The Escape" and "The Summer of
Love"; *Midwest Quarterly*, "This is Your Gift"; and *The Sewanee Review*, "Song of the Powers."
    I especially want to thank Frederick Morgan and Paula Deitz of *The Hudson Review*
for their extraordinary support of my work, and Ron Koury of the same magazine for
his editorial help.
    Several poems in this book also appeared in *Land Without Grief*, a chapbook pub-
lished by Jones Alley Press of Colorado Springs, who also printed a limited edition
broadside of "Three Characters from a Lost Home." Thanks to Joan Stone and Sally
Hegarty for their fine work.
    A videotaped performance of "The Country I Remember," read by David Mason
and Laurie Wigtil, directed by Robert Schieffer, was broadcast on Prairie Public
Television on August 4, 1995. The poem was also performed by actors Kelly
Bertenshaw and Jim Stowell at The Great American History Theatre in St. Paul,
Minnesota, on October 23, 1995. The author wishes to thank Kathy Friese, Richard
Zinober and Ron Peluso for making that performance possible, and the Moorhead
State University Foundation for financial assistance. The same university provided
Faculty Release Time during which some of the contents of this book were revised.
    "This is Your Gift" was set to music and performed by Diana Segara at the Kerry
International Summer School in Ireland, August 1995. "Letter to No Address" was read
on Kerry Radio.

CONTENTS

I

II

For My Parents:

Evelyn Mason Brueggeman
James Cameron Mason
Claire Tangvald

and

Arthur Brueggeman (1915–1990)

I

THE COUNTRY I REMEMBER:
A NARRATIVE

> The campfire embers are black and cold,
> The banjos are broken, the stories are told,
> The woods are cut down, and the young grown old.
>
> W.H. Auden, *Paul Bunyan*

How We Came This Far

Mrs. Maggie Gresham, Los Angeles, two years
before her death in 1956:

The rattle and sway of the train as it clattered across
leagues of open grassland put me to sleep,
and I dreamed of Illinois where land was flat
and safe as anything that I had known.
I woke to find my sisters counting bones
on the prairie, and the sky beyond our smoke
was a dusty blue. We were heading west.

Papa slept beneath his broad-brimmed hat
and Mama sewed—she made the pinafore
that I was wearing. I knelt beside my sisters,
watching land go by from the wooden seat
like waves of a great ocean being tossed.
The snow had melted, and everywhere it seemed
were bones like cages with no birds inside.

We'd packed a cheese, a stack of pies, boiled ham
and jars of fruit preserves from our old farm.
The Indians would come aboard each stop,
begging for food, or selling calico.

In Cheyenne my sister Beatrice had croup
and Mr. Kress said to take some snuff with lard
and spread it on her throat—that cured her quick.

I remember looking out the train at night,
trying to count the dark shapes passing by
and seeing our faces pressed against the glass
like children looking back from another world.
I thought of bones in the embrace of weeds,
of Indians who vanished on the prairie,
of hills that swayed and rumbled like our train.

Had my Papa brought us to this empty place
in desperation? I watched his regal head
nodding on his chest, the long V of beard
flowing over his crossed and worsted arms.
I was the happiest child when we had left
the farm, but now I prayed
the night would not destroy us like the lost.

The poets told us that this land was new
but, though I was a child, I understood
it was as ancient as the word of God,
and we were like those wandering tribes of old;
no one had chosen us to travel west,
and it would serve no purpose for a girl
to question choices that her parents made.

I knew this fear would always follow me
wherever I went, that I was not real,
that no one really lived who bore my name.

The lamplit face upon the swaying glass
was all that I would ever know of truth.
When Mama snuffed the lamp, my other face
retreated to the land of passing shadows.

§

Next morning while our mother brewed our tea
on one of the coal stoves inside the car,
I felt us being hauled away from dawn
by force of steam, and heard my Papa speak
to Mr. Kress of wars that he had fought in—
they whispered so we children wouldn't hear,
and Mr. Kress no longer looked so jolly.

The war that made my Papa look so old
happened in Tennessee and in Virginia
long before my sisters and I were born.
War had taught my Papa to stand up straight.
War gave him his heavy cough each winter,
but we had never heard the things I heard
intended for the ears of Mr. Kress.

Then the tea was ready and the two men
roused us children for another day.
They knew the reason we were heading west
and understood the bones out in the grass.
They were like prophets in the holy book
interpreting the tablets for the tribe,
and we the children of an Israel

unspoken for except by all the dead.

§

The Kresses said good-bye to us out west.
From Portland we went inland on the river—
strange to be pointed toward the east again
as if our path were the snake that eats its tail.
After the rivers and mountains of our journey
the land we traveled through was dry and grassy,
and Papa kept his stories to himself.

He paced the riverboat, nodding at land
because he'd known some part of it in youth
and memory had made him bring us back.
Washington Territory
looked for all we knew like the Holy Land,
and 1880 was our year of hope
and we believed our Papa understood

what made the wind blow steady off the buttes.

§

Papa bought the ranch near Pomeroy
and he had the first-ever frame house built
in the Blue Mountains, which were more like hills.
There the little savagery of childhood
ran its course—we tried to be young ladies,
but winters were hard; we had to dig out,
keeping the axe and shovel in the house.

Snow drifted over fields and filled the lanes,
so Papa built a sled with a wagon box
and we rode to school over the tops of fences.
I had a dog named Buster who got lost
in a blizzard. Some of the men rode out
but saw no sign of him until that spring
a passing cowboy said he'd seen the bones.

Time passed. I thought of Buster on the prairie
and how we came this far from Illinois,
counting the bones beside the railroad tracks.
The snow had gone. The hills were turning green
and I was tired of all our little chores
on Papa's ranch, tired of staying home
with only a slow spinsterhood before me.

We came this far, and maybe I could go
farther on my own. Papa had slowed down
but wandering was in my blood—and his—
and he would have to understand my going
and how no place had ever been my home.
As long as I was moving there was hope
that I would find the place we all had sought—

even my Papa, back when he was young.

Cobb's Orchard

Lt. Mitchell shortly before his death
at Pomeroy, Washington, in 1918:

A hungry army's enough to spook the dead
the way it marches on without a sound,
only the clatter of our gear and wagons,
a noise of hoof and boot hemmed in by hills.
We were in McCook's force, pushing south,
the western flank of Rosecrans' three corps
butting General Bragg from Chattanooga.

Two days out of Goldsboro we ran short
of rations, feeding off the countryside.
The first day without food my boys made do
with coffee. After that my colored man
went out with a sack to gather what he could.
He caught up when we camped on Willow Creek,
a heap of elderberries all he'd found.

"We'll feast on 'em," I said. The 79th
had gathered hay enough for all our horses.
My company had elderberry juice,
cooked in kettles and coffee pots for supper.
My Captain said, "Men, shake out your haversacks
for crumbs," but there wasn't enough to feed a bird
and the men fell quiet, looking at their boots.

Charley was my colored man. He'd no horse
so I gave him fifty cents to hire one,

told him to find our regimental sutler
back with the main force over the divide.
Next morning, Charley and the sutler came
just as the bugle sounded us to march,
and brought two wagons loaded down with food.

His people still were slaves, but Charley was free
and came to work for me not long after
we formed the 79th in Illinois.
The boys had voted me Lieutenant 'cause
I'd done a bit of fighting in the west—
bought me a fine sword I was proud to wear.
Charley kept it polished till it gleamed.

I meant to ask him where his people were,
but never did. He couldn't read a map.
He told me once he didn't want the Rebs
to catch him, fearing they would sell his hide.
When we got whipped at Chickamauga, Charley
had no place left to run. He just stood still
and waited for the Rebs to get a rope.

But all that hadn't happened when he rode for food. . . .

§

Two more days with no supplies. We foraged
off the countryside as best we could.
I saw a Negro with his hat in his hand
ahead of us on the run. Charley and I
rode out to stop him. I wanted to know

what he was running from and if he knew
of anything out here to feed my men.

"Yes, Suh," he says, pointing with his old hat.
He told of an orchard, five acres of fine
ripe peaches that belonged to Senator Cobb.
"They's a rise and a ridge with a basin 'tween the two
and right over that's a gulch and over that
they's peaches enough for all you Yankees there."
I rode back and reported to my Colonel.

"Colonel," I says, "perhaps you can recall
an ex-Senator Cobb who owns the land
not far over that rise." I said I wanted
men and wagons to feed the regiment.
He let me go with twenty-one infantry,
an able Sergeant, sixteen cavalrymen
for front and rear guards, the wagons and mules.

We found the orchard right where we were told,
and I got the boys to cut their way to it,
building a road so the wagons could cross the gulch.
We laid our ponchos underneath the trees
and shook loose peaches so ripe you could smell them,
filled two wagons, keeping one on reserve
for any vegetables that we might see.

It was a warm September day. The smell
of grass and dust and peaches hung in the air.
Except for our harvest sounds, all was silent.
As far as we would see, no people worked

the fields. All the men were fighting, I guess,
and who knows where the women hid themselves
with two great armies out upon the land?

I took my mounted men across the hill
to a large mansion, where I hollered, "Hello!"
A fat man stepped out who was full of whiskey.
"We have twenty-five thousand starving men,"
I told him. "If you have any food to give
I will receipt you for it. Swear loyalty
and you'll get paid."
                              "Damn your receipt," he said.

The boys unslung carbines to do him in
but I said we were only here for food
so let him be. The fat man cast an eye
up the ridge to my right, and there I saw
a mess of graycoats coming over the rise.
I gave the order and we spurred our horses
down where my men had backed the empty wagon

to a corn crib. They had filled it with white corn
and I said, "Boys, the Rebs are after us!"
By this time I could hear their rebel yell
and thought a hail of minié balls* would hit us.
You never saw a mule team move so fast
as ours did, but I knew the Rebs were faster.
When we reached the road I had the wagons stop.

* *minié balls*. Named for French Army Captain Claude E. Minié, who in 1848 perfected a
bullet that could be rammed down the barrel of a rifled musket with greater ease than pre-
vious ammunition. These .58 caliber bullets left particularly bad wounds in men unlucky
enough to be struck by them.

I had the teamsters run their mules to cover
and ordered the boys to line up double quick
in groups ten feet apart. The Rebs had stopped
on the hill behind us. I drew my sword
and let the sunlight catch it so they could see
the Yanks were ready for them. My Sergeant was
a big, hot fellow who wanted to fight.

He knew the Rebs could hear him so he said,
"You folks want our grub, you'll have to come on down."
We saw that they were not ready to come;
they couldn't tell how many men I had.
Our pickets had some trouble the day before,
so I said, "Boys, give 'em hell." I had them fire
four times a minute for just three minutes.

The vidette cavalry rode up to see
our fight in time to watch the Rebs back off.
My men let out three cheers for the enemy.
Then we were on our way with wagons full,
two of peaches, one of corn and brandy.
The shooting warmed us up enough; I knew
the boys on foot stepped lighter than before.

Looking up, I saw birds fly between the trees
and disappear amid the tangled branches.
They seemed to follow us and share our joy,
lighthearted creatures made for a bit of song.
It took me back, I don't mind telling you,
as if this road led to my family's farm,
turned west, and opened to the vast beyond.

§

But soldiers do like honey. At some bee stands
those who'd stolen a nip of brandy tried
to rob the hives; they had a worse skirmish
with those bees than the one with Johnny Reb.
You never saw so many stung-up fellows
raising dust as they leapt about the road.
I ordered a nip of brandy all round.

Half a mile on we saw hogs in the brush.
I rode to a nearby house and there found
an old couple dressed in homespun, sitting
in the shade of an oak. I asked about the hogs.
"Yes, Suh, we've seven if you count Old Betty."
"We have twenty-five thousand starving men,"
I told them. "I'll receipt you for those hogs.

If you're loyal, you'll get paid. If not,
you'll get nothing."
                              "Hell, Yankee," the old man said,
"I'm as loyal as you are. I love the old flag.
Mother and I just have to play rebel."
Mother said, "Let them Yankees have the hogs.
The Rebs will take them if you don't. Let them
have all but Old Betty, save Old Betty."

The boys went out and shot down six hogs,
all but Old Betty. I figured they were
two hundred pounds apiece, five cents a pound,
and wrote up a receipt for the old man

who touched my hand and wished me a safe journey.
Back then our farm in Illinois was much
like his, and it made me think of my wife and child.

We got back safe with peaches, corn, honey,
hogs and brandy, halted where the Colonel
rode out to meet us behind the picket lines.
"Did you have any trouble, Mitch?" he says.
"Yes Sir," I said, "we skirmished with some bees."
The men were a great sight, so badly stung
we had to laugh, but they ate well that night.

Some of the corn was cooked by laying ears
in the hot ashes of the campfires, some
shelled and parched in the kettles of our cooks.
We slept all right, but next day had new orders
to cross the river and march to Sand Mountain—
we were on our way to Chickamauga.
Supplies were never sent to that old couple,

which has bothered my mind for all these years.

All Houses Are Haunted

Mrs. Gresham:

Some nights in the Palouse the moon-blue sky
was windless, stars adrift in its forever.
No one knew how often I left the ranch
and walked alone out to the luminous fields,

my nightdress trailing in grass like spun silver,
and lost myself in meditation there
before the day I really left for good.

When you leave a place it is more beautiful
those last few days, the earth will open up
secrets you never guessed at: the hushed grass,
the bluish cottonwood that seems to wait
and breathe with you in solitary union.
Alone on a hill at night, you can feel
the world was made for us to listen to.

Other nights I thought us the accidents
of a sorry God, or worse. Overcome
by silence, I could feel the planet whirl
like a crazy bronco bucking through space—
the best that we could do was grip the saddle.
Those were the nights I felt I would be crushed,
my family would wake and not recall me.

Who was I but the girl who read Longfellow
to her Papa when his war-damaged eyes
no longer focused on the page, and when
no men came by to listen to his stories?
My sisters loved the poets too, but I
was the one who read aloud. I understood
always that I was here to be a voice.

"All houses wherein men have lived and died
Are haunted houses." Yes. And looking back
across the fields, so wide awake around

my Papa's house, I saw how fragile love is,
how easy to uproot from any place,
how hard to plant again. I was a voice,
an echo, if you will,

though nothing echoed in that open land.

Acoustic Shadows

Lt. Mitchell:

We climbed Sand Mountain and could see the dust
raised by Bragg's army beating a retreat.
That night we saw the flash of cannonfire
but didn't hear a sound. "Acoustic shadow,"
the Colonel called it, hillsides all lit up
like summer lightning, but only a drizzle
hissed and the men were too dead tired to hear.

Then Bragg vanished. We were ordered back
to Chattanooga where we suffered more:
no rations, and water in short supply
so men drank from horse and mule tracks and wrung
out moisture from mud stuck to their ponchos.
Six miles out of Chattanooga we lay down
like dogs in the road beneath a long cliff.

More than a mile east we could see a belt
of timber marking the river's course, the smoke
of rebel campfires drifting from the trees.

They had chosen this for their battlefield.
During the night we heard them move to the ground
below us, bivouac so near we smelled
tobacco sweet enough to drive us mad.

Next morning the big guns that woke us up
pounded a short ways up the line. Charley
brought me a cup of water he had scavenged.
"No more of them acoustic shades," he said,
and I could see he knew we were in for it.
The guns thudded and rapped like heavy mauls
driving a stout post deep into the ground.

I told the Colonel of a trick I learned
in the Indian campaigns out west. The men
could bite a cartridge end and suck a third
of the powder out. So stimulated then,
they would not think of their thirst; we'd be firing
at close range and would not need a full charge.
He sent the order out along the lines.

At daylight an orderly came from Chattanooga:
"Men, get out of the road," he said. "No cheering."
Then General Garfield and his staff rode through
the lines, twelve officers who raised their hats
to every color they passed. They all set
forward in their saddles just a little
and made a sight. We formed ranks in their wake.

When my brigade came under enemy fire,
the Rebs shot from breastworks of brush and rock.

The 79th Illinois marched up
on top of them before we shouldered rifles.
We opened fire at thirty steps. Crazed with thirst,
our desperate men knelt down and kept on firing,
stood and fired again into the thick smoke.

We fought our way toward water, all our guns
rattling till they made a single roar,
minié balls shredding through the grass and leaves
and boys dropping wounded to their knees.
We could see the timber belt, reached water
short of the river in a marsh. The men
threw off the scum and drank the puddles dry,

and found the spot alive with wiggle-tails.
We heard the rebels yell, and we yelled back,
though many of our boys were badly wounded.
For a moment the shooting stopped. My hand hurt
from gripping the hilt of my sword so tight,
but I was in one piece and saw to my men.
A fellow from Illinois fell next to me

and lay stone dead, staring up at the clouds,
blood thick in his beard. I saw where the ball
had ripped open his guts, and in his last
moments he had torn his tunic open
searching for the wound, now packed with dead leaves.
I just had time to dismount and close his eyes
and mutter a Lord have mercy over him.

But rebel sharpshooters still lay ahead
on a hill, their bullets cutting through the trees.

Men were hit, horses were hit, and finally
a ball grazed Colonel Butler on the shoulder,
so he shouted to Captain Clark, "Get rid
of those pesky fellows, will you?" I told
the Captain, "Give me eight men. We'll climb up

that rock a quarter mile off and take
a shot at them." I got more volunteers
than I could use, chose eight from my company.
Colonel Butler said, "Mitch, dislodge those men,"
I saluted and inquired of Captain Clark,
"What's your pleasure, Sir?" The Captain said,
"Kill the long-haired devils where you find them."

We pulled off our blue coats and haversacks,
advancing from the Pennsylvanian line.
"Go get 'em, boys," said one. The Captain there
only shook his head: "You won't come back."
At the base of the rock two poor skirmishers
lay stone cold where the sharpshooters dropped them.
We crawled ahead, our pantaloons grey with dirt.

Then Tommy Wenn, a noble young churchgoer
from home, said, "I'll pass over," and ran up.
The skirmish line kept firing to make work
for the sharpshooters, so Tommy could pass.
We all passed over in like manner, I last,
and with good cover climbed up the hillside
a mile, came out to the sharpshooters' rear.

They fired at our reserves a mile away,
dropping bullets, as it were, from the clouds.

We advanced to spitting distance from the first
sharpshooter. I told Tommy Wenn, "You wait
till he lifts up to shoot, then fire at him."
Tommy got the first man with a clean shot
through the head. We had to lay the body

over the splattered brains to hide the sight.
Tommy stayed in the dead man's barricade
to shoot the ground at intervals and fool
the Rebs while we went on to do the next.
We killed six in this fashion, with one left
atop a gulch. I took Jesse Peterson:
"Now Jesse, take your time, but you get him."

Jesse lowered his rifle and said, "Lieutenant,
I'm afraid my gun won't reach him from here."
We went further, till Jesse found a rock
to rest his rifle on. He cocked the gun,
and just as the rebel's hairy head appeared,
Jesse let him have it. We didn't bother
to gather up that sorry soul's remains,

but took the first six rifles back to our lines.
The soldiers raised Tommy Wenn on their shoulders
and gave three cheers for Mitchell and his men.
The Colonel sent a dispatch bearing praise.
But while we did our job the rebel guns
blew up the roadside cliff two miles away,
killing some of General Garfield's staff.

I'd been in a shadow and I did not hear it.

Leaving Pomeroy

Mrs. Gresham:

Running away is something children do
and I was not a child. Though I ran out
those many nights, I always came back home
by dawn to see to it that Papa was fed
and help out Mama any way I could.
She used to tell me I should have my own life
and there were plenty of men about who'd do.

My sisters snatched up half the able men
in Pomeroy. Oh, I had offers—eight,
to be exact—but I had wanderlust
like some have measles; anyway, my brother
lived for the ranch and would take care of it,
so I made plans to see my parents settled
and strike out for the world all on my own.

By 1900, Papa found the ranch
harder to manage. We bought the big house
in Pomeroy so we could take in boarders,
left the wheat and cattle in William's hands,
though Papa went back any day he could
to mend his fences or repair his tools
or just to wander in his memories.

Some people have no gift for growing old.
Though there were days Papa could hardly breathe,
the old cough coming back, his eyesight poor,

though his hair and beard had long been white,
he still had the bearing of a younger man
and thought himself a soldier, and so we
were forced to soldier with him all those years.

My sisters and I were quite small, like Mama,
with her brown hair and eyes, and some said we
were pretty, admiring our clothes and manners—
my parents made sure we were well-behaved—
and now with all the grandkids coming by
it seemed as if the Mitchells of Pomeroy
had justified their travels.

I was almost thirty. I had said no
enough to good men that my sisters thought
I'd lost what little brain I had. I helped
our Mama cook and clean for boarders, men
who came for harvest work, or to punch cows.
By autumn I had told them I was leaving.
Mama sat down, frozen, in the kitchen,

and that night I made dinner by myself.

§

She was ten years younger than our Papa was,
and a much sturdier Methodist than he—
she used to organize camp meetings back
in Illinois, and taught her children prayers.
The world we knew in childhood was all God's,

but somehow as we grew God slipped away,
or didn't hold us as He used to do.

The war hurt Mama too. Her brother died,
no one knew just where, and after that
her father had no use for Southerners
and never spoke to one. Papa, of course,
loved people no matter who they were,
wanted every stranger in Pomeroy
to stay at the Mitchell house and hear him tell

his stories about escape from Libby Prison.
My parents were unlike each other in
the way they bore the burden of the past;
that day I took the train
I saw Mama cry for the first time ever;
Papa simply ordered me to write
and stood beside her, waving, as I left.

I see them both receding on the platform,
Papa in his suit and watch-chained vest,
Mama veiled as if for someone's funeral,
the whole town growing smaller till I saw
it wasn't a town at all, but a few trees
nestled in the grass of a great dry land
growing so much wider by the minute

that suddenly I feared what I had chosen.

Boyish War

Lt. Mitchell:

"All wars are boyish, and are fought by boys."
My daughter read that to me years ago—
Maggie, the one who left for California.
We weren't all boys. I was thirty-three
and I knew older men in uniform.
But we fought like boys. You know what I mean.
We bragged and laughed when we weren't terrified.

And I saw schoolkids torn apart by bullets,
their heads bashed in by Confederate rifles.
And I saw Yankees do a thing or two
to make those people hate us all their lives.
But in those days I couldn't waste my pity
on men who broke our union.
There was a fire in me that made me fight.

Not anger—no, nothing like that old Greek,
Achilles, who we read about at school.
I don't think I could ever really hate,
or could even understand Abe Lincoln's cause.
He was from Illinois and he was ours,
and we elected him our President,
and when he asked for volunteers, I went.

§

We were the right flank at Chickamauga,
and never saw the center of the fight

where Longstreet charged a gap in the Union lines
to give his West Point roommate, Rosecrans, hell
at great cost to both sides—many thousands
killed, wounded or missing in two days—
and set the stage for Missionary Ridge.

After we killed the rebel sharpshooters,
my men and I stayed out on the high ground
for the view. We saw another old boy
dressed in a butternut suit, dodging and shooting
half a mile off, but didn't have the heart
to do him in. He only had a shotgun
and didn't kill a living thing I saw.

Near sundown seven stands of rebel colors
moved toward us from the Chattanooga side.
In the confusion of our fight that day,
as ranks were scattered and reformed in smoke,
the picture changed. I told my boys to move
back to the Pennsylvanian skirmish line
as fast as their tired legs would carry them.

I told the Pennsylvania Colonel, "Sir,
there's seven stands of colors waving there.
They are for us, as we're inside their lines."
We found my captain with the Illinois
telling the men tall tales beneath a tree.
In the dim light he asked, "Mitch, is that you?"
I passed him the bad news to give our Colonel.

Our order was to hold the rough terrain
at all hazards. The Army never thought

a second Lieutenant could get tired or hungry
and I was given charge of Company F
whose captain had been wounded in the morning.
I cast an eye for Charley, my colored man,
hoping he'd stayed arrears with our supplies,

but heard about his fate a few days later.

§

The land was full of hollows, broken fences,
and we were like regiments of blind men,
blades before us, poking for the enemy.
Suddenly we were firing at their lines.
When they fired back we ordered, "Down to cover!"
Damned if they didn't pass right over us.
I ordered the boys to change, front to rear.

When we raised up I saw that we were stuck
between two rebel battle lines. The boys
in gray came running up and shouted, "Captain,
hand us your sword."
                              "I can't see it that way,"
I said. A rebel parried, but one of mine
bayonetted him and was in turn thrust through
with a bayonet and dropped down at my feet.

The fellow who called me Captain bled and moaned
and died pretty quick. Though I couldn't see
a damned thing, I sensed the fight was over.

I slipped my sword inside my pantaloons
so when they captured us I walked stiff-legged.
A rebel Sergeant much in sympathy
asked me where I was hit and offered help.

I told him I fell off my horse and cracked my knee
and he said, "Suh, I b'lieve that hoss was shot."
Looking back, the whole thing seems unreal,
the way we walked along like two old friends.
Scattered shooting broke the night behind us,
though I could see that most of us were taken.
The rebels built a bonfire out of rails,

and in the firelight brought more prisoners in.
My Colonel hugged me like a baby, said,
"Mitch, you were worth your weight in gold today."
He said he knew that I could handle men
and would make Major if we could escape.
But we were told to sit down in the dark
and held at gunpoint all that weary night.

§

Next morning we were searched for valuables.
I hid my jackknife down inside my shoe;
a ring I made from California gold
I wrapped in tobacco, pretending it a chew.
The officer in charge strolled up to me
and said, "Now I will have to have that sword."
He waited, arms crossed upon his tunic.

I didn't want to be dishonorable.
General Hull in the Revolution, who
commanded two of my own ancestors, broke
his sword in the ground when taken prisoner.
"I'm not going to make a Hull of myself,"
I said, but made no move to give it up
and offered silence to this officer.

It only made him madder. He detailed
three men with loaded pieces to take aim:
"Suh, I do not want to use harsh measures."
I saw those barrels pointed at my breast
and thought of Mrs. Mitchell and the baby,
saw my chance for escape would have to wait,
unbuckled my sword and handed it across.

I felt just like twenty-five cents. They asked
whether my name was on the sword. It was not.
They regretted that it could not be returned.
I wished that I had given it to the rebel
sergeant who saved my hide the night before,
but now I had to watch this officer
replace his rusty saber with my own.

Then I felt like six-and-a-quarter cents.

The Country I Remember

Mrs. Gresham:

By the time the train pulled into Portland, I
knew there was no one who could save my life
but me. Now I was twenty-nine years old,
a spinster with a love of poetry
and no money, experienced at cooking.
Portland was a brick city on the river
with some degraded shanties for the poor.

Fishermen, lumberjacks and prostitutes,
bartenders and bankers rambled her streets,
and I saw quickly it was rougher than
the frontier village that my Papa knew.
And wet. I swear it rained all winter long,
the smell of fish and cut wood everywhere.
I spent a week just wandering the streets,

looking for work to pay for my hotel,
but what could I do? I couldn't bring myself
to sing in a saloon with sawdust floors
or join the mission at the riverfront.
I saw that I had lived with family
to fortify me far too many years,
and I would have to learn to live alone.

The hotel keeper, Mr. Jenkins, must
have pitied me; he offered me a job,
first as kitchen help, then behind the desk

keeping his accounts. It paid my room and board
and something extra that I set aside—
my first Christmas away from home I sent
small presents to the folks in Pomeroy.

I had a private room on the first floor,
a bed and dresser and electric light
for reading so I didn't strain my eyes.
"It rains across the country I remember."
That was a line from Trumbull Stickney, read
in another room some other, later year,
but I remember feeling it in Portland,

closing my eyes and burrowing in the sheets
to listen to the water streaming down
the walls outside, the brick streets rushing
all that dark water downhill to the river
where it kept on going silently to sea
and clear across to China. I was alone.
I was alone and it was more than I could bear

to lie there listening to that driving rain.

§

Maybe that is why we go on talking,
always trying to show someone we're here,
and look—I have a past just like you do,
a stream of words that fills the empty night
and sweetens troubled dreams, or so we hope,
and tells us not to linger long on bridges
staring at all the water passing by.

I thought my whole ambition was to make
the past and present come together, dreamed
into a vivid shape that memory
could hold the way the land possesses rivers.
They in turn possess the land and carry it
in one clear stream of thought to drink from
or water gardens with.

I learned that I must first talk to myself,
retelling stories, muttering a few
remembered lines of verse, to make the earth
substantial and to bring the sunlight back.
I thought of all the bones out on the prairie,
of Mrs. Kress who came aboard our train
in a tight corset, so my sister Beatrice

said she looked like an ant. I thought of land
that flowed far out beneath us like a river
turning the dead face-upward in the wake
to talk to us of all their ruined lives
in a Babel of tongues. And then I knew
I worked to keep these troubled dreams at bay
and keep the talking dead from drowning me.

"It rains across the country I remember."

§

When spring came, Mr. Jenkins offered me
employment of another kind—a ring
along with all the duties of a wife.
He'd put his best suit on when he proposed

and I could see why others might have faltered,
fearing nights alone, but I was expert
at saying no and hardly knowing why.

I told him I would move to California.

Sojourners

Lt. Mitchell:

Someone told me that mankind always moves
from east to west, but in my day I've traveled
back and forth like a saw blade cutting wood.
When I was young I worked my father's farm,
but when at twenty-one I became a man
I left the farmwork and the biting flies
to drive an ox team out to Oregon.

That was back in 1852.
The journey took three months, a lot on foot.
I saw whole households strewn across the prairies,
all extra furniture discarded when
we reached the bluish foothills of the mountains.
We added graves to those beside the trail
and traded worn-out oxen as we went.

At Cheyenne we picked up new wagon ruts
and followed them northwest across the hills
until high forests closed us in, the trail
full of growth we had to cut with axes.

I'd never seen such streams—what the poet called
"The cataract of death far thundering from
the heights"—clean as Heaven, shot with rainbows.

I'd say the mountains raised my spirits up
more than any sermon ever did.
I met a man who wintered there and looked
a granite carving brought to life by magic.
Everywhere I went I wondered how
it looked before it fell to human eyes,
before some storyteller called it home.

The mountains were home only to the gods,
according to the Indians, and I,
well I was young and I believed so much
the world was mine for taking.
                                        At last we came
to Portland, a town of log cabins then.
Never was a land so full of rain—
the ground soaked it up and squished when you walked.

The sky was always like a tattered mist
and most days keeping dry was hard to do,
but the woods were full of game, the lakes of fish,
and you could feed yourself with hardly a sweat.
I met a man named Barley who would fish
the river with a gill net like the natives,
hauling in salmon half as big as a man.

Joe Barley had come from Massachusetts
not for gold, but because he had no life

to hold him in the east. I fished with him
one fall, learned how to build an alder fire
and keep the coals banked low to smoke the fish.
I said I'd travel south to California;
Barley had a notion of coming too.

We panned for gold on the Humboldt, cut wheat
with cradles in the Sacramento Valley
the hottest month I ever labored through.
We packed mules to prospect in the country
near Mount Shasta and were lost for three days.
We heard about the Indian fights up north
and how the Rogue and Klamath picked a fight,

and then we joined the Oregon Mounted Dragoons
in 1856. They made us Corporals
and I recall my horse was so damned slow
I was always catching up. That's how I missed
half the fight in the Siskiyou Mountains,
rough, thick-wooded hills with lava outcrops,
where I saw Barley die, pierced by an arrow.

It wasn't more than three men we were chasing,
four months after Colonel Wright was murdered.
Some said Wright had raped an Indian girl,
some that she was the one who ate his heart;
a few of our men were still hot for revenge.
Barley, who had ridden out in front,
was nearly dead of bleeding when we found him.

They'd taken his horse, left Barley in the sun
where we found him sitting up, swatting flies
and watching his own blood cover the grass.
"Mitch," he said, "I wish I'd stuck to fishing."
The Indians were hiding in the rocks.
Our men dismounted and were loading rifles,
shooting into the rocks, then running up.

The one they caught that day regretted it.
I was too busy holding my old friend
to notice all the noise on the hill above.
I must have looked up, though,
and when my eyes came back to Barley's face
the life had left it. I dug Barley's grave
and carved his name on a marker made of wood.

We had a preacher with us who could sermon:
"For we are strangers before thee," he said,
"and sojourners, as were all our fathers:
our days on the earth are as a shadow and
there is none abiding." He read some more
but those are the words that I remember most;
they made me miss the farm in Illinois.

I knew my father must be getting old.

§

I thought of sojourners in the train's darkness,
hauled with other Union men to Richmond.

I fretted about the way I lost my sword,
and the stench of packed-in men hardly helped.
There wasn't room to tend the wounded ones
whose moans, together with the chugging train,
dragged through our days and nights of traveling.

The Chickamauga prisoners were kept
at Libby Prison down on Carey Street,
beside the James River and Lynchburg Canal,
a brick warehouse built to hold tobacco
where now a thousand Union officers
huddled on its upper floors and learned
to sleep like spoons when nights grew long and cold.

"Well, you'uns look like we'uns, quite a little."
That was our greeting from the Reb commander,
pointing out his cannon aimed at the walls,
his soldiers eager to shoot all Yankees
attempting to escape. But I don't think
the man was evil; that night he fed us
beans and meat, never so much food again—

his men were hungry too, quite a little.

The Blacksmith

Mrs. Gresham:

Howard Gresham pried a "yes" from me
by sheer stubbornness. He was a strong man
and he simply wore me down. I'd lived alone

some years and thought I'd always live alone,
but fell for him as though I were a girl.
He wasn't a poet any more than I,
but he reminded me of some old verses:

"His hair is crisp, and black, and long,
    His face is like the tan;
His brow is wet with honest sweat,
    He earns whate'er he can,
And looks the whole world in the face,
    For he owes not any man."
Those were lines my Papa used to love.

Howard was a real blacksmith for ten years
who worked his way out west from Minnesota.
When I met him he owned a dry goods store
in Santa Rosa, where I worked as a cook
in a restaurant. He had these strong arms
from wielding a heavy hammer all those years
and looked much like the fellow in the poem.

He'd come by the restaurant once and seen me
going in to work, and then he came back
and asked me on a picnic in the hills
outside of town. It was summer. "For, lo,
the winter is past, the rain is over and gone;
The flowers appear on the earth. . . ." Those words
were dancing about in my head that day.

The hills of Santa Rosa had turned golden.
Sometimes they reminded me of the Palouse,
but winter wasn't hard in California.

I loved to take long walks outside of town,
so I said yes, and then I think I laughed
and said, "For, lo, the winter is past," Howard
knew the verse and finished speaking it.

Right there in the restaurant that drew me
to him in a way I'd never felt before.
He knew the verse, though he'd had little school
because his father died at Gettysburg
and he'd had to learn a trade. I said yes,
I'd join him on his picnic in the hills.
That night I thought about it; doubts came back.

I told myself my travels were not done.
I still had thoughts of Mexico and further
south if money hadn't slowed my progress.
I had an idea that I would write a book,
but I could never sit still long enough.
I hardly knew this man, but clearly saw
that I could settle down and live with him.

No, I'd think, to marry him is to betray
yourself. Look at all the women you've known
who wear a path from house to school to church,
yoked like oxen, milked like cows, and told
to be as pretty as the foliage;
as if the noise of children's not enough
they nurse the manhood of their husbands too.

I ranted alone inside my rented room,
rejected Howard half a dozen times

when all he'd asked me was to go for a walk.
And when I tried to sleep I thought of love
and thought he would be capable of it.
And then: why would any man want me?
I'm such an old maid, thirty-six years old!

The picnic was a Sunday I had off.
We dallied for a long time on the ridge,
talking about our fathers and the war
and what we hoped for, coming west. I thought
the kindness in his face was kindness earned
by hardship and a solitude like mine.
He was forty-five and still a bachelor,

kept from marriage by his work and travel.
His family were all dead but a sister
in Minnesota he wrote postcards to.
For our picnic he brought sandwiches and beer
and threw a blanket on the grass, and we
sat in the shade of a black elm and talked.
When he returned me to my room that night

I had a wire that told me Mama had died.

§

When you have gone away to help yourself,
a death at home is somehow more your fault,
as if you could have stopped it, made a mood
of happiness that would keep death at bay.
But I had not seen Mama since the day

she shrank beside my Papa as the train
pulled out—my last view of her, after all.

The train back home ran through the corridor
of rain to Portland, then by the river east.
I have never grown used to trains going east,
but the hills were familiar, farms of wheat
and standing herds out in the heat of summer.
All of my sisters were there, kids and husbands
with them, my shy brother and his new bride,

and Papa, standing on the platform, still
like a soldier, erect, his thinning hair
covered by a hat that matched his suit—
Mama would have bought him that and made him
wear it in the sun. He must have thought
she would see him buried in that suit, and now
sudden disbelief showed in his gaunt face.

Some of my sisters stayed at William's ranch
and let their children ride the horses. Papa
wanted me at the house in town, and said
he'd like to hear me read to him again,
which of course I did: Whitman on the war,
Longfellow and Lowell and Trumbull Stickney—
he liked that line of Stickney's on the rain.

Weather for a funeral could not be found
at Pomeroy in summer: dusty blue
rose over the steeple and the grassy buttes.
"We brought nothing into this world, and it

is certain we can carry nothing out."
The minister was old, and his voice faint:
"I will lift up mine eyes unto the hills. . . . "

The rustle of children filled the wooden pews,
and I heard their shoes on the floor, tapping
and scraping the Lord's floorboards, and I thought,
This is life going on, this is the form
of memory, the way our voices will remain.
I have avoided life too many years.
I have wanted to disappear, and now

at last I am ready for my life to come.

Rat Hell

Lt. Mitchell:

The winter of 1863 and 4
was hard on all the men in Libby Prison.
Men from Gettysburg and Chickamauga
huddled on the upper floors, but when
we cooked or had our dead to carry down
the Rebs let us tarry on the ground floor.
By Christmas we were planning our escape.

Maybe you've heard of Colonel Rose's tunnel.
I was one of the fifteen men who dug,
sworn to an oath we would not tell the others
for fear the word would spread. If officers

escaped we might release the thirty thousand
private soldiers on Belle Isle, and then march
any way we could for the Union lines.

It was almost more than I could do to wait.

§

I knew a Sergeant Brown of the 25th
Virginia, came on duty at midnight, who
gave us tobacco and a morning paper.
A few years ago in Wallace, Idaho,
I met a lady in a bank who said,
"Lieutenant Mitchell, my father's an old soldier.
I want you two old veterans to meet."

I was in Wallace visiting a daughter.
One night this lady brought her father by
and I thought him familiar by his bearing,
and he said, "Yes Lieutenant Mitchell, I
have given you tobacco many a time.
I was near court-martialled once for giving
a flask of whiskey to one of your wounded men."

If it wasn't Sergeant Brown! I visited
his home, and several old Confederates
came by, and we had a wonderful time.
We had a Southern meal in Idaho,
then cigars, and Sergeant Brown's daughter played
old songs we all knew on the piano,
as if no war had ever come between us.

§

There was a basement in the Libby Prison
called "Rat Hell," which was where we tunneled from.
In the Chickamauga Room we loosened floorboards,
slipped into the first-floor kitchen at night
and made a hidden hole behind a cookstove.
One of the men had rope and fixed a ladder,
sailor fashion, for us to climb down on.

We dug out from the east wall of Rat Hell,
hoping to make it past a vacant lot
to a shed attached to a towing company,
our one tool the knife I'd hid in my shoe,
a knife that still remains in my possession,
broken and mended, worn toothpick thin.
A hundred men depended on it once.

While digging, we could hear the guard above
in the lot call, "Three o'clock and all is well,"
and had to keep from laughing, though the work
was rough and men who dug were all half sick
from the stink of the box sewer next to us.
By day we kept a watchman concealed in ricks
the Rebs had stacked below, and all day long

that fellow felt the rats run over him
and gnaw his flesh. One fellow used my knife
to kill a rat and baked it nice and brown
and said he never tasted sweeter meat,
it was just as good as squirrel.

                              Once the tunnel
broke a small hole into the vacant lot,
so I crawled in to see what could be done.

I'm telling you, to crawl under the earth,
smelling a stink that nearly made you sick,
inching yourself along by pulling roots
and wriggling like a worm inside a grave,
you can't lie still to think of smothering
but let your mind go blank and concentrate
on the job, like a piece of carpentry.

When I poked through to moonlight in the lot,
wearing the burlap sack we used for work
to spare our uniforms, I knew at once
I had to hide that hole. I scraped some mud
from the ground above and packed it with my blade,
making the airshaft look like a rat burrow—
so I hoped. Anyway, they never found us.

But I came out all mud from head to foot,
knowing I had caught a chill. Captain Clark
and Major Hamilton helped clean me up.
I donned my uniform and climbed upstairs;
by the time I found my blanket I was sick,
my skin all clammy and my forehead hot,
and knew that I had been that sick for days.

                    §

I had bad dreams (and I am not a man
who dreams) of water boiling up from down
below, a shaft of moonlight turning it
to blood. I dreamed of cannonfire. One. Two.
The guns pounded like that. One. Two. Three. Four.
I saw my first-born buried on the farm
and prayed that I would live to see my wife.

I started coughing blood out of my lungs.
The rebel doctor said I had pneumonia;
when I heard that I thought I was a goner,
tried to sleep and stop the dreams from coming,
but when your fever's high like that, the mind
plays tricks on you. My breath came in great heaves
and the strangest dreams kept floating in my head.

The night they finished digging I recall
a dream of Mrs. Mitchell. As you know
she liked to keep things neat, and in my dream
she said I looked a mess. "Now Mitch," she said,
"you straighten out or I won't marry you."
I tell you, the woman never looked so fierce.
She frightened me so much I had to live.

"Now Mitch." It was the voice of Colonel Rose,
the night of February 9th. The boys
had thrown their blankets down by me, he said.
"Now Mitch, this is good-bye. I hate to leave
a man behind, but you know we can't wait."
He looked a kindly bear with his great beard,
and I said I was glad to see them go.

§

More than a hundred men escaped that night.
The Rebs arrested their own guards, and would
have shot the bunch of them, but someone found
the tunnel, made a Negro boy crawl through
and saw where he came out inside the shed.
When they assembled all the men to count,
I was carried down cocooned in blankets,

and carried back, still moaning in my dreams.

The Children's Hour

Mrs. Gresham:

This morning on the radio I heard
a robbery on Rosecrans Avenue
in Hawthorne got some old gentleman killed,
all for fifty dollars. And then I thought,
"Rosecrans Avenue," and it all came back,
how my Papa had fought in Rosecrans' army
at Chickamauga in 1863.

And when I was a girl I used to sneak
into the grown-ups' room, invisible
behind a chair, and listen to his stories.
Before he died a fellow wrote them down.
I have them in a box somewhere, with all
the letters Howard sent when we were courting
in Santa Rosa after Mama died.

No one ever wrote down Mama's stories.
And here we are in 1954.
I'm the last of the Mohicans, just about.
Ida died not long after Papa did.
Beatrice died in 1922.
William was killed by a horse in 1930.
Agnes died in a car wreck in Seattle.

Olive's living still in Pomeroy
and likes to call me on the telephone
to ask about the weather. She came down
to visit not long after Howard died
and went to see the houses of the stars.
My nieces and nephews are all grown up
and like to see Aunt Maggie in L.A.

They say to grow old without children is
a curse, and sometimes I believe it's true—
to have so much to say and no one here
to say it to. I have a niece who comes
and takes me for a drive out by the sea
and shows me how the city's spreading out
clear to the mountains.
                              When we first came here

the place seemed almost as wild as Big Sur.
Howard had the store in Bakersfield
till 1928 when he retired
and we moved to Inglewood. All those years
we saw our chances for a family
go by until there was no chance at all.
Our baby didn't live beyond four months.

I tried to summon up my old belief
or find some verse that would relieve the pain,
but life won't always come when it is called.
We heard about the store in Bakersfield
and Howard saw the move would do us good
and I said, "Yes, my people always move
when staying in one place is killing them."

In Inglewood we used to have a shop
where we sold flowers, and I remember watching
young men stammer over roses for their girls
and thinking maybe I had let it all
go by too quickly. I had some regrets,
wondering if old age would be as dry
and dusty as the hills.

Depression, war, rations and hard times.
Howard wouldn't let me dwell in the dark.
That's what we had work and laughter for,
he said, to pull us out and land us on
our feet, and keep our dead from sinking us.
He was like Papa in that way, knowing
always how to plant his feet on the ground.

The other day my niece, Alyssa, brought
her two young girls along and we had dinner
near Pacific Avenue, then drove out
to the beach where the girls could have a swim.
They were such lovely things, with their long hair
and much more freedom than I ever knew,
the way they flirted with the boys out there.

Alyssa rambled on about her job
selling real estate after her divorce,
and while I listened, all at once I heard
the hoofbeats of the surf come pounding in.
I thought it was the voice of memory
crashing and flowing down across the earth,
and underneath, like roots that probe for water,

and I was moved by everything that moved.

Eighty Acres

   Lt. Mitchell:

In 1866 my son was born,
William Thomas, partly named for the Rock
of Chickamauga. My father, getting old,
wanted me to stay on and care for him,
so I built a good frame house next to his
and worked our eighty acres in Edgar County,
and raised my children up with Mrs. Mitchell.

We'd cattle and fowl, corn and timothy.
The children walked two miles to school, and had
a fine teacher who taught them proper speech.
I like people, as you know. Anyone
passing by was invited in to dinner.
One time a walleyed man and his daughter passed
and stayed for three years, helping on the farm.

The daughter taught my girls to sing folk songs:
"Froggie Went A-Courting," "Little Brown Jug."
In 1876 my uncles came
to see my father once before he died.
He was ninety then, but when they came
he rose from bed he was so glad to see them.
My father died in 1878.

Mother had passed on twenty years before.
I was damned near fifty myself, and saw
it might be my last chance to move out west.
This country's always on the move. Sometimes
if you don't want to carry a great weight
you drop it and walk away. America
is made by those who want to change themselves—

my father did the same when he came out
from Boone County, Kentucky, years before.
Now my wife was thirty-nine, but healthy.
We sold the farm with all our furniture
at auction, tools I sometimes wish I'd kept,
loaded up our five daughters and one son
and took the train from Paris, Illinois.

That was the last my wife saw of her folks.

§

They kept me seven months in Libby Prison,
part of the time so sick I thought I'd die,
the rest malnourished, hardly able to walk.

The Rebs recaptured nearly half the men
who crawled out through the tunnel. Some they kept
below in cages where they fed on rats.
The whole business was a bit discouraging.

The more the war went on the meaner it got,
and we were glad to hear the Union guns
start in on Richmond. One day a Reb guard
came upstairs where we were sitting, and said,
"What are you boys doing?" He looked half-crazed.
I told him that as far as I could tell
we were prisoners of war. He was new,

just a kid, looking at us lying there:
"You fellas ever get anything to eat?"
I said we had a ration every day
and it was pretty good but not enough.
There was a bucket of beans and some cornbread
brought up, and the boy looked at it and said,
"Is that the kind of stuff you have in here?"

He said he wouldn't touch it for it was full
of worms. I told him, "I don't see the worms."
I ate my ration, but the rebel boy
wouldn't eat. Next day I guess he was hungry
and he said he couldn't see the worms either.
The Confederates there ate the same rations
we did, just like they were prisoners too.

§

A whole mess of new prisoners arrived,
but Richmond was done for. They lined us up
outside, where I stood a while in the shade.
A chaplain came up and said, "Lieutenant Mitchell,
why don't you fall in line?" I said the ground
was too rough for me to walk upon. "Why,"
he said, "it's level as a floor out here."

But to me the whole city seemed to wobble.

§

They shipped us first to Macon, Georgia, then
to the jailyard in Charleston, South Carolina,
where we saw the Union batteries lobbing shells
into the burning city; so they pulled us out,
giving us rice and cabbage leaves to eat,
to a place called Camp Sorghum, near Columbia.
I don't mind telling you conditions there were bad.

More sick and crippled men I'd never seen,
and many died. Some days I felt oppressed.
It seemed that if we stayed there we would die.
When I think back to all those muddy graves,
sometimes I recall a line of poetry
my daughter read to me: "O how can it be
that the ground does not sicken?"

The world was sick and winter on its way.

§

Maybe the Rebs were just too tired to watch us.
One night half a dozen of us bolted,
struck out across a field that once had been
full of cotton, for you could see the rows,
and into trees that scattered water on us.
It was damn foggy and we ran all night
only to find we'd circled back to camp!

So we started the opposite way and came
to a house with a lady out fetching water.
One of the men had a grey suit and went
to her and said he was Confederate,
and she said, "I will divide what I have
with a Confederate soldier," and gave
him biscuits which he carried back to us.

While he was in the house a sow came by
with four or five pigs. I was accurate
with a rock, but I threw and threw at those pigs
and never hit a one. I couldn't see
distinctly any more from months of hunger.
We walked at night without a star for guide
till we saw there was someone on the trail:

a Negro came along on his way back
to a camp where he was working as a cook.
We told him we were Yanks and he was scared
but said, "God bless," and took us to his cabin.
His people there had little food, but gave us
bacon and cornbread, let us get some sleep.
They said we had been moving south and might

catch up with General Sherman in Augusta,
sixteen miles away. For men as tired
and worn out as we were, that was good news.
In all my rambling days I never felt
a sixteen miles so distant. We left at daybreak
so we could see our route across a swamp,
threw our shoes away as they were almost gone,

and made ourselves some moccasins from the hide
of a dead cow we found mired in the mud.
But we would never make it to Augusta.
We ran straight into a rebel picket line
where Morgan's men were shouting, "Halt. Halt. Halt."
One was so excited his rifle shook
at us and I thought he would shoot. He said,

"Give us fair play, Yankees, give us fair play."

֍

This is an account of my experience,
though much is left out: the end of the war
and sorry death of Mr. Lincoln, months
in hospitals spent getting my strength back,
return to Edgar County, Illinois,
where Mrs. Mitchell, who had had no news
for quite a time, was glad to see me home.

I had little enough to show her for
the trouble of my being gone. The sword

I bought in Washington for the last parade
was not as fine as the one that I had lost
at Chickamauga. She told me our first-born
died while I was gone. No one knew the cause
and she had kept her grief for my return.

I've told these tales before, but wanted someone
to set them properly on paper, now,
in case my mind in old age starts to drift.
They say that when you age the distant things
are closest, and some days I find that true.
Sometimes I think of Oregon and young
Joe Barley, and the lonely way he died.

Sometimes I think of all the blood we've spilled,
but thinking that way only brings bad dreams.
It's good to have the young ones coming by
for visits, though Maggie never had her own
and she's still living out in California.
Mrs. Mitchell died twelve years ago.
It came sudden. The doctor said a stroke.

Forty-eight years together, she and I,
and most of it was work. A fellow can't
put into words the help she gave us all.
Not only the children. There were bad days
when glumness got the better of me, she said,
"Mitch, you've come too far to give up now."
I talk a lot, but some things I can't say.

I'm getting used to living here in town.
This is my home. This is my home because
I say it is. I told you about my life
so you would know how this place is my home.
I knew I'd come back like a boy in love
and build my wife that frame house, room by room.
I knew that one of us would choose a grave.

And I will rest there when my time has come.

II

EL RIO DE LAS ANIMAS
PERDIDAS EN PURGATORIO

No one recollects where the Spaniards died.
A rescue party found their armored bones,
thought their souls estranged from the love of God;
so the river was named and flowed on past,
bearing no knowledge of its wandering spirits,
cupped to baptize newborns in the valley.

My people came here when the coal mines started,
fed their young on Rockefeller's scrip.
In late summer, stilled by the weight of leaving,
the hot, exhausted railyard seems to ache.
The red-haired boyhoods of my father's clan
become the stuff of anecdotes with coffee.

In boarded businesses and weed-cracked streets,
few recall them. Under a secret sign,
the eye and compass, ancestors lie buried,
but I have never been to see their graves.
My people's time beside the Purgatoire
was brief—far briefer than our scattering.

We called her ghost
because she was pale and rarely appeared;
thin as a broom, she made a sickly host;
her fungi-fingered
house leaned as her great trees would lean, wind-tossed.

Crossing from school
the bridge on the gully full of stinging nettles
where boys with knives were known to fight, and girls
broke every rule,
we scanned her pulpy porch boards for a ghoul.

With subtle age
like petals of a wilted peony,
slumped gray timbers released her from their cage
so soundlessly
that we still chattered past them on the bridge.

One day her house
had vanished in cascading weeds and vines.
We hadn't known the woods would come so close,
that life declines
caught up in brambles underneath the boughs.

THREE CHARACTERS
FROM A LOST HOME

Cedar:

Though they drill and count my rings,
mark Columbus near my heart,
a thousand other happenings
elude discovery from the start,
and I have secrets deep enough
only the pale blind taproot knows,
worming far beneath the duff.
The uplift of my trunk bestows
in swooping terraces a green
intelligence to catch the wind;
invisible, it can be seen
when I am shaken and I bend
and almost let my branches fly.
I grow unmoving till I die.

Water:

No one can record my travels;
under snowcaves, through the heather,
my body stretches and unravels
downward, though a change of weather
floods or evaporates my strength
until old rocks like balding heads
settle their debate at length
along the ragged riverbeds
and I rejoin the gallery
of clouds adrift above a lake,
blown back against effrontery

from yet another stubborn peak
to fall in quiet squalls again,
and wait for my unravelling.

Woodsmoke:

I'll make your eyes tear up
and take you back in time,
blue smoke over water
thinned by summer rain.
A table ringed by laughter
leaves no one to complain;
I make the room feel warm,
the mind remember sleep.
What will-o'-the-wisp recalls
its own birth as it fades?
My burning home enthralls
with all its leaping blades,
while I drift out of stone
into the woods alone.

I went to sea in the Summer of Love
in a boat with my Boy Scout troop.
That summer I was only twelve,
our boat a rusty sloop.

The island where we spent a week
lay twenty miles from home,
but in our minds we were refugees
from vaguely exotic doom.

A dozen boys who lolled about
on beaches, lied about girls,
stared at any passing yacht,
chanting the latest Beatles,

we liked the underwater voice
of "Yellow Submarine"—
all the DJs ever chose
to play in the afternoon.

Our scoutmaster, Mr. MacIntosh,
went quickly mad. He drank
from tidal pools and chased the fish,
his eyes would never blink.

The fathers who came to take him away
in a little trawling boat
gave our troop permission to stay
three days with no adult.

With no adult, what savages
we were! Our boyish lies
grew like grotesques, the vestiges
of epic ecstasies!

But sometimes Mr. MacIntosh
came back in our fireside tales.
The world of grown-ups seemed awash
in trouble; some took pills,

some gassed themselves in their garages.
Recalling those who were mad,
we poked our sticks in the campfire's ashes,
unaccountably sad.

(Later I read that the Summer of Love
was the summer of the damned;
sixteen thousand American boys
had died in Viet Nam.)

We dreamed after girls on the passing yachts
and waited in the shade,
and when the adults came back in boats
to rescue us, we were glad.

On the wharf at home we bought ice cream cones,
shook the sand from our shoes.
We shambled back to casual lawns,
Monday meetings, other friends,
the feeling that summer never ends
and we would never lose.

Sundays they went skiing on the mountain
while others knelt in church. So undisturbed,
he played beneath cold blizzard vaults of heaven;
attendant snowflakes hushed the spoken word,
and no one's word became a sacred book
with strings of parables explaining why
the wind in branches sounded like a brook
or unseen giant who exhaled the sky.
Riding home, he dozed in the damp wool smell
and murmur of grown-up talk inside the car,
as if the universe were play and dreams,
and there were nothing that resembled hell
on earth or elsewhere—just oncoming dark
probed by descending cars with lighted beams.

The wind that stripped the birches by the lake
dusted the first snow on her hollow gaze,
then warmed her slender limbs for no one's sake.
Hunters who found her stood by in a daze,
kerchiefs on faces, till the sheriff came.
No records ever gave the girl a name.

Anonymous as leaves along the shore,
where waves fall into lines until they freeze
and winter drifts against a cabin door
and change comes quickly on a southern breeze,
the birds will tell us nothing of her worth
whose small bones left no imprint on the earth.

Mine, said the stone,
mine is the hour.
I crush the scissors,
such is my power.
Stronger than wishes,
my power, alone.

Mine, said the paper,
mine are the words
that smother the stone
with imagined birds,
reams of them, flown
from the mind of the shaper.

Mine, said the scissors,
mine all the knives
gashing through paper's
ethereal lives;
nothing's so proper
as tattering wishes.

As stone crushes scissors,
as paper snuffs stone
and scissors cut paper,
all end alone.
So heap up your paper
and scissor your wishes
and uproot the stone
from the top of the hill.
They all end alone
as you will, you will.

In summer insects clouded over the pond
and all was still, except for the hound barking
at swallows that flew circles through the air.
The boy was wet from kneeling in the grass
to look inside the leaves, and played a game
with a willow switch that he had broken off,
trying to balance it in his open palm.
At the house, drawers and bedsheets hung on lines,
the old barn sweltered in its peeling paint,
velvet soil was disked, arching over the rise
to fields where his invisible father worked—
but as he played he balanced all of this
like the switch that wavered in his outstretched hand.
Even the high gibberish of geese heading south
was part of the great stillness at the pond.

§

Now the white lady with powdery stockings
and soft chest returns to the chair where he sits.
He doesn't want her blanket, he wants her breasts
unbuttoned, pushed close to his face, but she
pins his hands to the chair. "No, Mr. Berge."
They're always putting down his hands like that.
The white lady's gone, swinging her white rump.
The hound's run off with the switch in his teeth.
The man has lost count of the cars on the road
with their faint grinding noise beyond the grass.
He sees the stubble of an early harvest
next to corn rows leading to an iron sky
beyond the fence. Somewhere out of sight
fly squabbling geese. It hurts to lift his head.

They told him to lift his head and look up
at the woman in his room. No one he knew.
She was old. Whatever she cried about,
he couldn't fix it. "I can't fix it," he said.
"Where in hell has that hound run off with my switch?"
Over the rise where his father worked. "They got
a chain-link fence there now." But the marsh grass
still clutches the wet soil at the pond's edge.

When he stands he can feel his cold t-shirt,
but doesn't want the blanket on his chair.
Too much to carry and he isn't going far.
He shuffles down the lawn where the pond smell
grows inside him. Geese babble in wet clouds;
the summer's gone, faster than it ought to.
Sometimes the night comes out of the tall grass
just beyond the fence that helps him stand
so he walks along it, smelling the earth

so full in his nostrils, so still the day
he balanced the switch upon his open hand . . .
His hands on the fence are thick, patchwork creatures,
red over lifted bones.
Of course the woman who cried in his room was Agnes.
He knew it well before he said her name,
but couldn't explain the blackbird in his skull,
the way it passed its wing across his eyes
and wiped out all the years.

He stands at the fence and tries to remember Agnes
peeling an onion in the kitchen sink,
wiping tears on her sleeve. He has seen

those walls with roses on them many times
but doesn't recollect who lived in them.
They move away as if the house were jacked up
and hauled off on the bed of an old truck.
Faces come and go in the moving rooms
but he can't remember any of their names.

§

All the sudden he's taller than the fence.
The railroad ties for flowerbeds are piled
almost close enough. He steps down, rolls one
off the heap. Smell of creosote and pond.
Summer smell of ditch grass and cut soil.
The ties roll easy down against the fence
and he can stand above the topmost bar.
With a long *Oh God* he rolls over the top,
lands on his back in the tall grass, looking up,

and there they are—geese in a ragged V.
They squawk like an unoiled flywheel. "Give it
some oil," he says, and laughs with his hurt ribs.
The fence stares down on him from a long ways
but the lady in white can't grab him now,
and anyway, he's heading to the house,
over the furrows to the drawers and bedsheets
where the hound has run.

He starts around the pond,
but the earth is weaker than it used to be.
The mud sticks to his shoes, he falls and stands

with wet black circles on his trouser knees—
just like that day he balanced on his palm
until the old man came back from the fields
and tanned his hide for some chore he didn't do.
He feels the switch come down across his back,
the tears squeezed from the edges of his eyes.
Nobody tells him why this has to happen.
What did I do to you? he wants to know,
but his old man won't say a single word.

His arms feel wet, it has begun to rain.
There are no geese, there are no swallows here.
His father rages and his mother waits
down in the earth where he is kneeling now.
He cannot see the laundry on the line
because the wind is bending the tall grass
and bending the willow branches over him.

Now the fence is gone, there are only fields
of black soil, corn rows leading to the sky
which lowers darkly, driving down the rain.
The cars go by more quickly on the road.

That's when he knows the hound is long, long dead,
and that the woman crying in his room
cried for him. She could help him find the barn,
but he no longer can recall her name,
and anyway, the soil is numbing him
with cold. It's easier to lie down here
and wait for the whipping that will surely come.

Downcast thermometers record one truth
of winter, though the clear light hints of spring.
The furnace blows a warming reverie
where I drop anchor somewhere in the woods
with a girl I haven't seen for twenty years.

I find the pond secluded in the park,
filled by a waterfall beside a bluff
where we held hands and jumped, yelling love,
laughing to find ourselves alive again
and young as always, touching each other's skin.

Tonight the temperature is due to fall,
an arctic stillness settle on the prairies. . .
The years slow down and look about for shelter
far from forests and far from summer ponds:
the mind ghosting out in a shoal of stars.

Who is the lover sleeping beside you?
How can the gentle curve of a hip
or shoulder awaken to guardedness?
The long shape of the lover beside you
dreams like the river of waking and sleep.

The river of breath flows out through the boughs
and turns them to shivers outside the house.
The river of spring comes over the land,
melting the snow all night so the ground,
though haggard, is ready again for love.

What is this mystery? What is this sorrow?
Touching your lover in sleep, on a journey
you cannot follow? This is your gift.
This is your emptiness, rising and falling.
What has been given? What has been lost?
Breathe with the body beside you and know.

LETTER TO NO ADDRESS

Another winter holds the town at bay,
inward-looking as the river freezes,
dark water glazes over, and closes.
Home from work, I mark the narrowing day.

For hours this letter weighed upon my mind,
a secret hauled from underneath the ice,
kept from others till I could find a space
for lines I have no notion how to send.

The past I would recapture is a land
whose contours changed the further I moved out,
years from cedars where we built a hidden fort
and you were the scrappy leader of our band.

Brother, I want to map the old hardscrabble
places we ransacked, bluffs or high above,
leaping from stone to stone with a wild love,
the ache of play erasing all our trouble.

As boys we followed parents up the pass,
switchbacking marmot rocks through Devil's Club.
We hunkered under peaks from the weather's stab,
but storms could not prepare us for divorce.

That route, chosen without our consent,
abandoned children in a wilderness
where breaking voices met hard silences,
fear the one emotion never spent.

Perhaps to conquer fear, I followed you,
the distant older brother, when you traveled.
Like you I married, though my love unraveled
far from the woods and mountains that we knew.

And you were not a boy on that last climb.
The trouble you carried upward was your own,
The glacier where you fell as white as bone.
When I recall that instant I go numb.

I live in a world too full of elegies,
and find no compensation in these lines,
nor can they map where memory begins
its restoration under winter skies.

A MOTION WE CANNOT SEE

We found the path somewhat as it had been:
heather and rock of an alpine meadow
ringed by peaks like giants in a myth
we never learned; all our lives
we had played among them, and perhaps
our grief was payment of an unknown debt.

Perhaps the strange mist
caused us to question the path,
but our boots made a familiar sound
on the dirt runnel; the gray rocks
and stunted firs were congregated
as before.

We couldn't say why we had come,
two living brothers and our father
whose hands were like ours
and like our brother's hands,
bones and hair so much like ours,
flesh of our silent flesh.

I saw the place where we had cupped
the ashes, letting them blow
and drift over the heather.
A year of snow and snowmelt later
what could be left of him,
so utterly possessed by mountains?

Yet after the year of weather
tiny pieces of my brother's bone
still lay in clefts of rock.

We found them under our hands,
cupping them once again in wonder
at what the giants left us.

Since then I have not gone back
to hold my brother's bones. The prayers
of blizzard and snowmelt have him now,
and time flows down the mountain like the ice,
a motion we cannot see,
though it bears our blood almost forever.

David Mason grew up in Bellingham, Washington, and has lived in Colorado, Alaska, New York, Pennsylvania, and Greece. Since 1989, he has taught at Moorhead State University in Minnesota. His first full-length collection, *The Buried Houses,* was co-winner of the 1991 Nicholas Roerich Poetry Prize, and has been highly praised for its humanity and breadth. His translations, essays, poems, and stories appear regularly in such magazines as *The Hudson Review, Poetry, Grand Street,* and *The Sewanee Review,* and his work has been widely anthologized and translated.